Your Free (

I wanted to show my appreciation tha
so I've put together a free gift for you

If you would like to have it
send simple an empty email with the subject
"Send me the free gift" to:

contact@goodlivingbooks.com

I know you will love this gift.

Thanks!

Larry Todd

University of Birmingham School
12 Weoley Park Road
Birmingham, B29 6QU
0121 796 5000

Content

Introduction 4
   Becoming a Faster Runner 4
Chapter One: Preparation 5
   Running Journal 5
   Setting Goals 5
   Maintaining a schedule 5
Chapter Two: Strength Training and Jump Training 7
   Strength Training for Runners 7
   Plyometric Training for Runners 13
Chapter Three: Cross Training for Runners 24
   Benefits of Cross-Training for Runners 24
   Cross-Training Exercises 25
Chapter Four: Flexibility for Runners 27
   Yoga: The Secret to Flexibility for Runners 27
Chapter Five: Extra Tips for Running Faster 44
Chapter Six: Running Nutrition 46
   Nutrition Essentials for Runners 46
   Eating Pattern for Running Days 47
Chapter Seven: Maintaining your Motivation 49
   Tips for Sticking with fitness Goals 49
Chapter Eight: Running Injuries and the Simple Secrets for Avoiding Them 51
   Runner's Knee 51
   Shin Splints 51
   Achilles Tendinitis 52
   Plantar Fasciitis 52
   Hamstring Injuries 53
   IT Band Syndrome 53

Heel Pain 54
Chapter Nine: Training Programs for Running Stronger and Faster 55
Choosing the Right Training Program for your Fitness Level
.... 55
Training Programs 56

Introduction

Whether you're a beginner or a seasoned runner with a few marathons under your belt, it's likely that you want to become a stronger and faster runner. Running more efficiently and faster is a goal for many people. When you are stronger and run faster, it means that you can cover more ground in a shorter amount of time.

Becoming a Faster Runner

While jogging or sprinting may make you a better runner, it alone may not make you a faster runner. Generally speaking, runners tend to get so preoccupied with running as many times as they can per week, that they forget to supplement this with other training methods, which would actually boost their speed and strength more than running alone would. There are three main components to becoming a faster and stronger runner, which many people neglect:

1. Strength Training
2. Jump Training
3. Flexibility Training

When you combine strength training, plyometric training, and flexibility training with frequent running, you will become a faster and more efficient runner. What's also important for becoming a better runner is tracking your progress, setting goals, and maintaining your motivation. If you can combine all of these elements, both physical and mental, you can become a faster and stronger runner, and meet your fitness goals while doing so.

Chapter One: Preparation

To become a stronger, faster runner, you must prepare and have a plan of action in mind. Jumping into running with no clear goal, schedule, or aim in mind, is a bad idea. By planning and preparing, you will become a quicker and more powerful runner in a shorter space of time.

Running Journal

Before you start out running, make sure you purchase a running journal. Your running journal will allow you to document your workouts, keep track of your running schedule, and track your running progress and achievements. When you keep a journal, you can also see what type of workouts suit you best, and what types of training programs gave you the most benefits.

Setting Goals

Before you start your new running regimen, you need to set yourself a goal, or several goals if you're feeling ambitious. Think about what it is you want to achieve. Becoming stronger and faster is a goal for most runners, but you need to create more specific goals if you want to succeed. Do you want to be able to run a mile in four minutes, or conquer a half marathon? Write your goals in your running journal. When you write down a goal, you are much more likely to achieve it.

Maintaining a schedule

Without a set schedule, it's very unlikely that you'll achieve your running goals. Each week, ensure that you set yourself a running schedule. Ideally, you need four to five days per week to dedicate to your training. With work and family commitments, it can seem though to fit in training. However, everyone can fit in time before and after work, and during the weekend. Try to be disciplined and stick with this schedule. If you feel the temptation to skip a run, then look back at your goal to keep you motivated. Even skipping one day can ruin all the motivation you've set for yourself.

Chapter Two: Strength Training and Jump Training

Strength training and jump training can both make you a stronger, faster, and more efficient, runner and even reduce the amount of injuries you pick up.

Strength Training for Runners

One of the main secrets to becoming a stronger and faster runner is strength training. Running requires you to drive forward to gain speed and momentum, but most runners neglect strength training and instead, they focus solely on cardiovascular exercise. While cardiovascular exercise may be important, it alone won't make you a stronger or faster runner. Every week, you need to incorporate strength training into your workout routine.

Best Strength Exercises for Runners

1. The Plank

Requiring strength and balance to execute properly, the plank is an excellent exercise for runners. It works all of the muscles in the body, and stimulates the core in particular. By doing the plank, you'll strengthen your core muscles and with a stronger core, you'll be a stronger runner.

The plank is also an easy exercise to implement, as it requires no equipment. To do the plank, you first need to get into the pushup position, and then place your forearms on the floor, so that your arms are bent at a 90 degree angle with your palms flat to the floor. Then, simply hold this position for 10 seconds.

2. Lying leg raises

Working your core, and your hips, the lying leg raise is an ideal exercise for runners. To be a strong and fast runner, you need to have a strong core. Lying leg raises are fairly simply to do, as they require no equipment.

To begin, lie on your back. With your legs together, slowly lift both legs off of the floor, until your feet are pointing straight up at the ceiling, and your body and your legs form a 90 degree angle. Then slowly lower your legs back down to the floor.

With this exercise, your abs should be doing the work to lift your legs up, so if your back hurts, you are doing the exercise wrong. When you are doing leg raises, make sure that your lower back isn't arched. It should be flat against the floor. Pause briefly at the bottom, about an inch from the floor, and then rise back up to the starting position. Ensure that you keep your body in a straight line throughout.

3. Lunges

Lunges work almost all of your leg muscles, making them the perfect exercise for runners. Lunges can be done using your bodyweight or free weights. To complete a lunge, stand up straight, ensuring that your shoulders are back, your chin is up, and your upper body is straight. Then with one leg, take a step forward. Next, lower your hips, until one knee is on the floor, and both knees are bent at a 90 degree angle.

4. Bulgarian split squat

Bulgarian split squats are ideal for runners, as they work most of your leg muscles, as well as your glutes. While they are a little more difficult than some strength exercises, they are fairly easy to perfect after a little practice.

To complete a Bulgarian split squat, stand in a lunge position, and then rest the end of your back foot on something that's about two feet high, like a box. Then, like you would with a regular squat, lower your hips straight down to the floor and bend the front knee, until your thigh is parallel to the floor. Then, slowly rise back up into the starting position.

If you are new to strength training, then make sure you start out slowly. Begin by mastering just a few exercises at a time, and don't over-train. For runners, strength training is only necessary two times per week.

Plyometric Training for Runners

When you run, by nature, you primarily use slow twitch muscle fibers. By introducing plyometrics into you routine you will awaken the fast twitch fibers in your legs, which means that you will fully maximize the muscles you recruit when running.

More muscle recruitment means more power and more power means being able to push off faster and harder with each stride. A more powerful, faster stride means better running times.

The goal of any runner is to achieve faster and better running times. Most people feel that the obvious way to improve is to run more, but this isn't the case. Alone, running more frequently won't make you a faster or better runner. Running too often can be bad for your joints, it's tough to fit into a busy schedule, and it doesn't necessarily make you stronger or faster. This is where plyometric training is key.

Plyometric exercises will increase your explosive power, and will make you a much faster runner.

As plyometric exercises are explosive movements they must only be implemented after you have been following a solid strength program for at least four weeks, and you have a solid foundation built. A little goes a long way with plyometrics so make sure to listen to your body and increase the workload gradually. You should begin with easier exercises at first and then build it up over time.

Running is essentially a form of jumping. With every stride you aim to push-off the ground with force, while utilizing the ankle's mobility and trying to increase stride length with each stride. Runners who train this movement through plyometric training often improve their efficiency and, therefore, their overall performance.

Check out the plyometric exercises below and remember start easy and build up. Quality over quantity is key, 8 perfect reps are easily more beneficial than 12 poor ones.

1. Skips/Bounding

Choose a distance of perhaps 30 meters and skip to it. With each skip, you should be light and graceful. Aim to get as much height and distance with each skip as possible. The distance is secondary to the movement itself. The movement, rather than the distance, should be your focus. Bounding is essentially the same principle, but instead of a skip it is an exaggerated running motion. Again, focus on height and distance with each stride.

2. Ankle hops

Hop into the air, keeping your legs straight throughout, and use just the power of your ankles. Do not allow your knees or hips to aid in the movement. Again, you are looking for a fluid graceful movement, with as much height as you can.

3. Squat Jumps

Squat Jump

Start by standing with your feet shoulder width apart and your arms down by your sides. Bend at your hips, and then lower into a squat, ensuring your knees don't travel past your feet.

When your fingers touch the ground, you know you are in the bottom of the movement. From here, explosively jump up and try to get as much height as possible. When you land, make sure you have your legs slightly bent, to absorb the impact. Go immediately into you next rep.

4. Broad jumps

To begin a broad jump, stand tall with your feet shoulder width apart. Then bend at the hips and drop into a partial squat. Next, explode forward with as much force as possible, extending with your arms as you do. Distance is the goal here. As above, land softly with your legs bent.

5. Jump lunges

To execute jump lunges, you first need to stand straight, with your feet shoulder width apart. Then, step forward into a lunge position, and then explode into the air, and switch your feet as you do. Your back leg should now be in front and your front leg should now be in back.

Chapter Three: Cross Training for Runners

The term cross training is often mentioned by runners, but many people aren't quite sure what it is. Put simply, cross training, which is sometimes known simply as cross or XT, refers to aerobic exercise other than running, like cycling or swimming.

Benefits of Cross-Training for Runners

Overall cross-training offers runners a number of benefits.

1. Gives you an active break from running

As a runner, avoiding fatigue and the other problems that come along with over-training is paramount. While you want a break from running, you still want to stay active. With cross-training, you can give your body a break from running, but still get some form of exercise. Swimming and cycling are both low impact forms of exercise, meaning that they won't put the strain on your joints and bones that running does. While you'll be getting a break from running, you'll still be keeping your body active, your muscles strong, and your cardiovascular fitness level high.

2. Utilize all of your muscles

When you run, you tend to use the same muscles over and over again, like your calves and your hamstrings. However, with cross training exercises, like swimming, you use different muscles. By working different muscles groups, you will become stronger overall, and it will give your running muscles more of a chance to rest.

3. Keep your cardio fitness level high

Cross-training exercises all improve or maintain your cardiovascular fitness level, and therefore make you a better runner. The cardiovascular benefits of cross training exercises, like swimming, cross over to running really well, and further improve your skills as a runner.

4. It keeps you interested in running
Even if you love running, going for a run all of the time can become boring. Adding cross-training, in addition to strength training and stretching, can make your exercise routine more interesting, and keep you passionate about running.

5. Reduce your risk of injury
As mentioned earlier, you tend to use the same muscles when running, meaning that, as a result, your supporting and stabilizing muscles can be much weaker. By training your other muscles, you can help to balance out your muscle groups and make them all strong. Having strong muscles prevents many injuries.

Cross-Training Exercises
The following cross-training exercises are ideal for runners:

Cycling
Cycling increases your cardiovascular fitness and strengthens your muscles, making it one of the best cross-training exercises for runners. The benefits you get from cycling translate perfectly into running, meaning that a few sessions of cycling will likely make you feel stronger and fitter next time you go out for a run.

Swimming
One of the lowest impact exercises you can do, swimming truly is a dream exercise for runners. It keeps you in shape, and it won't put a strain on your joints. If you are recovering from an injury, swimming is the perfect exercise to do during your rehabilitation.

Walking
It's simple, low impact, and easy to fit into your schedule. Whether it's walking your dog, or walking to work instead of driving there, walking can keep you in great shape.

Rowing
Rowing is a fantastic form of cardiovascular exercise. While it's low-impact, it strengthens the hips, your upper body and

your glutes. Overall, rowing is a fantastic all over body workout, which will get you in great shape for running.

How often you incorporate cross training into your weekly exercise routine is up to you. Some runners like to use their rest day for cross-training, as it's so low impact, some runners like to mix it in with their strength training, but others like to devote a whole training session to it. It's really up to you, but later on, there are some training programs that recommend schedules for cross training.

Chapter Four: Flexibility for Runners

In order to be an efficient, strong, and fast runner, your body needs to be fluid and flexible. Unfortunately, running itself can causes tightness in the hamstrings, calves, and other areas of the body. Therefore, it can limit your mobility and make you a less effective runner. If you want to keep your body flexible and fully mobile, and avoid the tight muscles that come along with running, then you need to incorporate a stretching routine into your training program.

Yoga: The Secret to Flexibility for Runners

Yoga is one of the most important activities that you can do as a runner. Yoga poses are highly efficient at loosening your body, and making you more flexible overall. While it's great for increasing your flexibility, yoga also offers a number of other health benefits. It can reduce your risk of injury, reduce stress, improve your posture, and make you stronger. The following poses are excellent for runners.

1. Happy Baby

A simple, yet effective stretch, the happy baby is fantastic for opening up your hips and stretching your lower back. After running, the lower back and the hips can become tight, so this stretch is perfect for regaining flexibility in these areas. To start this stretch, you simply lie flat on your back on the floor. Then, bend both knees into the body, so that your thighs are parallel with your body, and then hold your feet with your hands. Then, keeping your arms on the outside of your legs, gently push down on both feet, and bring both knees down to the floor, near your armpits. Hold this position for 20 seconds.

2. Extended Wide Squat

Another yoga pose that is ideal for increasing the flexibility in your hips, and stretching your lower back, is the extended wide squat. To do the extended wide squat, stand up straight, with your feet slightly wider than your hips. Then, bend your knees and lower your hips towards the floor. Next, stretch your arms out in front of your body, and place your palms on the floor. Push your elbows into the inside of your knees, to further open up your hips. Hold this pose for 10 to 20 seconds.

3. Open Lizard

The open lizard pose is ideal for stretching your hips and your thighs, which makes it a perfect stretch for runners. To do the lizard pose, you simply get into a lunge position, with your right leg at the front. Then bring your left knee down to the floor. Place your hands on the floor, underneath your shoulders, and straighten your left leg out behind you. Your right leg should be bent almost at a right angle, and the outside of your right foot should be resting on the floor. Hold this stretch for 20 seconds and then repeat in on the other side.

4. Butterfly Pose

Fairly simple, but very effective, the butterfly pose is an ideal stretch for runners. It stretches your hips, thighs, and lower back. To get into this position, simply sit on the floor. Then, bend your knees and bring the soles of your feet together, until they are touching. Hold your feet together, and gently pull them toward your body, just slightly. Hold this stretch for 20 seconds. As you become more flexible, fold your body forward.

5. Arching Pigeon

Ideal for stretching the hips, your glutes, your back, and your lower abdominal muscles, the arching pigeon is a fantastic stretch for runners. Begin by sitting on the floor, with your legs bent and the soles of your feet facing each other. Then, move your left leg out behind your body. At this point, your right leg should be bent in front of you, so that your calf runs almost parallel to your body, and your left leg should be stretched out flat behind you, so that your left knee is pressed against the floor. Then put your hands on your hips and then gently arch your back. If you are not flexible enough to arch your back, and it hurts when you try to, then place your hands on the floor in front of you. Hold the stretch for 20 seconds.

6. Downward Facing Dog

Arguably one of the most popular yoga poses, and with good reason, the downward facing dog essentially stretches the whole body. To start the downward facing dog, get on your hands and knees. Your hands should be just in front of your shoulders. Then, walk your feet out behind you, until your upper body and lower body make a triangle shape. Then, spread your fingers wide and bring your chin into your chest, and look towards your navel. Hold this pose for 20 seconds.

7. Child's Pose

The child's pose stretches almost all of the muscles in your legs, making it perfect for stretching out tight running muscles. To complete the child's pose, knee down on the floor. Then, bring your upper body over your legs, so that your stomach is pressed against your thighs, and your head is on the ground in front of your legs. Then, stretch your arms out in front of you, with your palms flat on the floor. Hold this pose for 20 seconds.

8. Locust Pose

If you are a runner, the locust pose should be an integral part of your stretching routine. It can improve your posture and stretch your back. It's also a great pose for strengthening the neck, the arms, and the legs. To complete this pose, you simply lay on your stomach, facing the floor. Your hands should be next to your hips. Then, lift your arms, torso, and legs from the floor all at once, and hold this pose for ten to twenty seconds.

9. Dancer

The dancer pose stretches a wide range of different muscles in the body, from the thighs to the back. It not only makes you more flexible, but this stretch also improves your balance, which is essential for fast, efficient running. To complete this pose, simply stand up straight, and then bend the right knee back, behind you, and then with your right hand, grab your foot. Then, bring your right leg up behind you, using your right hand and raise your left hand up in the air, in front of you. Fold forward slightly at the hips and gently arch your back. Hold this pose 10 to 20 seconds. This pose requires the perfect combination of flexibility and balance, so it does take a while to master.

10. Upward Facing Dog

Another classic yoga pose that's beneficial to runners is the upward facing dog. It really opens up the chest and it stretches the shoulders and the back. To do this stretch, simply lay flat on your stomach. Then bend your elbows, and place your hands in line with the bottom of your ribs. Press down using your hands, and straighten your arms. At the same time, lift your hips away from the floor, and bring your chest up towards the sky. The tops of your feet should be pressed into the floor. Hold this position for 10 to 20 seconds.

11. Bridge

Ideal for building both flexibility and strength, the bride is a good pose for runners. The bridge stretches the back, the hips, and the fronts of the thighs. To complete the bridge, you simply lie flat on your back. Then, place your arms and hands behind your head, your palms should be flat to the floor, and your fingers should be facing towards your body.

Then, bring your feet in towards your body, and push up using your feet and hands, and bring your buttocks up towards the ceiling, until your body makes a curve. If you find this pose too difficult, you can try to do a half bridge pose instead. To do this pose, you simply leave your shoulders on the floor and your arms by your sides, and push up from your legs, and bring your buttocks up in the air.

12. Pigeon

The pigeon pose requires a fair amount of flexibility to fully execute. It's a fantastic stretch for opening up your hips and stretching the buttocks, back, and abs. Start by sitting on the floor, with your knees bent and the soles of your feet facing towards each other. Then, move your left leg behind your body. Your right calf should run almost parallel to your body and your left leg should be flat behind you and your left knee should be pressed into the floor. Then, place your hands out in front of you, with your palms flat on the floor. Fold your body over your front leg, as far as you can go, and then hold this stretch for 20 seconds.

13. Double Pigeon

Arguably the most difficult pose mentioned in this chapter, the double pigeon does require a slightly higher level of flexibility. This pose stretches the thighs, groin, and hips. To do this pose, get into the butterfly pose that was mentioned earlier in this chapter. Then move your right foot away from the body a little. Take your left leg, and position it in front of the left hip, so that your shin runs parallel to your pelvis, and the leg is bent at a 90 degree angle.

Then grab your right ankle and place it over your left knee, so that your shins are essentially stacked on top of one another, and are parallel with each other. Essentially, your legs should have created a triangular shape. Hold this pose for 20 seconds and then switch and do the other side. This stretch is fairly intense, so make any adjustments, slowly and carefully.

How often you do yoga is up to you. Some runners choose to do yoga poses as part of their pre-run warmup. Other people like to mix their strength training with their yoga, and many runners like to dedicate a whole workout session to yoga. Please remember that stretching takes time, and it should not be rushed. It's tempting to push yourself when it comes to stretching, as it does require some patience. However, if you try to take a stretch too far and you are not yet flexible enough, you can end up injuring yourself.

Chapter Five: Extra Tips for Running Faster

Strength training, flexibility, and plyometric training will all make you a stronger, faster, and more efficient runner. If you want to beat your person best for a mile, run a half marathon, or even run a full marathon, increasing your strength, power and your flexibility is what will get you there. However, there are also a few extra running tips that will make you a faster and stronger runner overall.

1. Watch where your feet are

Keeping an eye on where your feet are when you are running is important. For a fast, efficient run, you need to keep your feet directly beneath your hips.

2. Keep your head up

When you are running, you should be focusing on keeping your head straight. Look straight ahead, rather than up or down. By doing this, you keep your form good, and your run efficient.

3. Keep your arms at a 90 degree angle

Many people don't realize just what an important role their arms play during a run. Your arms keep your body stable, and assist your body in driving forward. If you want to increase your running speed, then you need to keep your arms bent at a 90 degree angle, swing them back and forth, and keep them relatively close to your sides as you run.

4. Keep your shoulders loose

Keeping your shoulders loose during a run is important for both your running form and your breathing. When there's tension in your shoulders or chest, it tends to cause poor posture, and limits your breathing too. When you run, keep your shoulders nice and relaxed.

5. Don't bounce

Bouncing too much during a run wastes your energy and it puts more of a strain on your lower body. Keep your strides light and don't lift yourself off of the ground too much. Your stride should be low.

Chapter Six: Running Nutrition

When it comes to running, your diet is just as important as your training. Putting the right food into your body can make you a stronger and faster runner.

Nutrition Essentials for Runners

Water

The body is made up of 70% water, making it essential for your health. How much water you need per day is widely debated. Generally speaking, the daily average recommended water intake for the average person is about two liters. However, some people, like those who are more active and those who sweat more, like runners generally require a larger daily water intake than the average person. On general days drinking two liters of water is recommended, but you may want to up this a little on tough running or training days.

Keep your meals nice and balanced

Eating meals that have a good balance of proteins, carbohydrates, fiber, and fat is essential. The carbs and the fiber will provide you with more energy, the protein will assist with building muscle and the fat will keep your body's cells and joints healthy. When it comes to fat, choose to eat foods that contain polyunsaturated and monounsaturated fats, rather than saturated fat.

Ensure you are getting plenty of vitamins and minerals

When you are running, ensuring that you get plenty of vitamins and minerals is essential. Vitamins and minerals assist your body in a number of important metabolic functions. If you are lacking in nutrients, it can have a real impact on your running speed and strength. Get plenty of fruits and vegetables, particularly green vegetables, like kale and broccoli, as these contain high amounts of vitamins and minerals.

Snack on healthy food between meals

If you want to keep your metabolism steady, and prevent an energy slump, then you need to make sure that you are eating snacks in between meals. When it comes to snacks, however, choose wisely. Many snack foods, like potato chips, are full of salt, sugar and saturated fats, all of which are bad for you in high amounts. By eating healthy snacks, like fruits, nuts, and vegetables, you can keep your energy levels stable throughout the day, and ensure that you are getting vital nutrients from your diet.

You don't need supplements… except one.

Supplements aren't necessary, especially if you are eating a healthy diet. Ditch protein shakes for chicken and turkey and swap vitamin supplements for fruits and vegetables. The only exception to this rule is glucosamine. It's very difficult to get glucosamine through your diet, as it is only found in shells, meaning that you have to supplement it. Glucosamine is excellent for maintaining healthy bones and joints, making it the perfect supplement for runners.

Eating Pattern for Running Days

On the days you run, your eating pattern needs to be slightly different, in order to account for your increased activity.

1. Before a Run

Eating a big meal a couple of hours before a run is a good idea. It will keep you full throughout your run, but won't weigh too heavy on your stomach. If you are going for a particularly long run, then have a small snack, like a banana before.

2. During a Run

Drink small amounts of water every fifteen minutes, to ensure that you stay hydrated. When you are running for longer periods of time, like more than an hour, you will need to drink a sports drink, which contains electrolytes and carbs, as well as offering hydration.

3. After a Run

After a run, you should be consuming a good mix of carbohydrates and protein. To get the best results from your run, ensure that you get protein and carbs into your system within 30 minutes of your workout ending. Good options for post-workout snacks are plain Greek yogurt with nuts and honey or chocolate milk.

Chapter Seven: Maintaining your Motivation

The physical side is just one aspect of becoming a stronger and faster runner. The mental side of running is just as important. Running requires a great deal of mental strength and discipline. As mentioned in the first chapter, having goals and keeping a running schedule are both important. However, setting running goals is not the hard part. The hard part is sticking with those goals.

Tips for Sticking with fitness Goals

1. Write it down

Writing down your goals and your fitness schedule makes you for more likely to stick with your new running regimen. When you lead a busty life, putting your workouts and runs into your schedule makes it easier for you to stick with your training program.

2. Track your progress

Using your fitness journal and a stop watch, keep track of how your running progresses. When you are training to become a faster runner, timing your runs using a stop watch is essential. For example, if you go for a ten minute run each Sunday, time how long it takes you, and make note of it in your fitness journal. After each run, write down everything you achieved, how far you ran, and how long the run took you. By writing everything down in your fitness journal, you can see how well you are progressing from session to session and from week to week. Tracking your progress allows you to see how well you are moving towards your running goals.

3. Have fun with your workouts

Running should be fun and enjoyable. If it's not, you'll likely become bored and frustrated and you'll do anything to avoid putting on your running shoes. To ensure that you keep your passion for running alive, make sure that you vary up your workouts. Incorporate cross-training into your routine and try running in different areas. Also, working toward a goal, and tracking your progress, as mentioned earlier, can also keep running fresh and exciting.

4. Make sure your Goals are Achievable

Often, people set goals that simply aren't attainable and then they feel disheartened when they don't achieve them. It's always better to break big goals down into smaller, more achievable goals. For example, if you have only ever ran a mile, and set yourself a goal of running a marathon in two weeks, this isn't something that you are going to be able to achieve.

Instead, break your goals down. For example, if you normally run a mile in 10 minutes, don't aim for a 4 minute mile immediately. Instead, aim for an 8 minute mile, then a 6 minute mile and then a 4 minute mile. By setting yourself smaller goals, you'll feel that you've achieved more and you'll be more likely to meet your larger goals.

5. Exercise with Others

Sometimes going for a run with someone else can boost your motivation and make things more interesting for you. Whether it's a friend, a family member, or a co-worker, getting a running buddy can help keep your motivation levels high.

6. Reward Yourself

If you've done well with your running goals for the week, and stuck to your training schedule diligently, then giving yourself a reward is a great idea.

Chapter Eight: Running Injuries and the Simple Secrets for Avoiding Them

Running injuries can slow you down and halt your progress. If you want to become a faster runner, and progress towards your running goals each week, then you need to prevent these common running injuries.

Common Running Injuries - How to Prevent Them

Runner's Knee

Runner's knee usually occurs when you've ran too much. An overuse injury, runner's knee, which is also known as Patellofermoral pain syndrome or PFPS, is when the cartilage on your kneecap becomes irritated or even worn down. Runner's knee has many causes. It can be caused by weak hips, glutes, or quad muscles, but it also occur when your kneecap is misaligned or if you have ran for an extended period of time. If you have runner's knee, you will generally feel pain or irritation when you walk up or down the stairs, sit with your knees bent for an extended period, or squat.

Tips for avoiding Runner's Knee

1) Slowly increase the miles that you run, and don't suddenly increase it.
2) Stretch before every run.
3) Strengthen your quads, glutes, and hips through strength training and plyometrics.
4) If you feel any pain after a run, lower your running mileage for at least a week.

Shin Splints

Shin splints is a generic term for pain along the shin or tibia. Shin splints are arguably, one of the most common injuries among runners, and are caused by many different factors. They can be caused by overusing or overworking your muscles, tendons, or ligaments, or by small fractures in the bones in the lower leg. People who have flat feet are also more prone to developing shin splints, as are those with weak stabilizing muscles.

Tips for preventing Shin Splints
1) Stretch frequently.
2) Avoid running on hard surfaces, like concrete, and choose softer surfaces, like grass and sand to run on, whenever possible.
3) Keep your muscles strong, by incorporating strength exercises into your training program.
4) Avoid over-training. It's tempting to workout seven days per week, but it won't help your running in the long-run. Make sure that you have at least two rest days per week.

Achilles Tendinitis
The Achilles tendon is what connects your calf to your heel. When running, this tendon is utilized. When this tendon becomes overworked, it can become inflamed. When the Achilles tendon is inflamed, it is called Achilles tendinitis. Signs of Achilles tendinitis include pain, soreness, stiffness, and irritation around the Achilles. When you have Achilles tendinitis, you will likely feel more irritation in the morning, and after activity. Tight calf muscles, overworking your tendons, or increasing your running mileage too significantly can cause Achilles tendinitis.

Tips for preventing Achilles Tendinitis
1) Stretch frequently, and ensure that you keep your calf muscles flexible.
2) Don't increase your running mileage too significantly.
3) Make your calves stronger through plyometric training and strength training.
4) Avoid repetitive strain on your tendons.

Plantar Fasciitis
Plantar Fasciitis is an inflammation of the tissue on the bottom of your foot, which runs from your heel to your toes. When this

tissue, which is called the plantar fascia, becomes inflamed, it causes a dull, bruise-like ache on the bottom of the foot. It's more common in runners who have a high arch. Generally, plantar fasciitis is caused by tight calf muscles, and over-running, but it can be caused by a number of different factors, like a weak core or tight hip flexors.

Tips for Preventing Plantar Fasciitis
1) Stretching, particularly calf stretches are ideal of preventing plantar fasciitis.
2) Run on softer surfaces when possible
3) Strengthen your core and hips.
4) Don't suddenly increase your mileage.

Hamstring Injuries
Many runners often experience pain in their hamstrings during or after runs. When you run, your hamstrings are what help to drive you forward, which means quite a great deal of pressure is placed on them. Pain or soreness in the hamstrings is usually caused by weak or tight hamstring muscles. When pain in the hamstrings becomes noticeable, it is best to stop running altogether.

How to Prevent Hamstring Injuries
1) Keep your hamstrings strong
2) Train all of your leg muscles through strength training
3) Don't overdo it with running. Your training should be slow and steady, and you shouldn't suddenly increase your mileage.

IT Band Syndrome
A ligament, called the IT, or iliotibial band runs along the outside of your thigh. It reaches from your hip to the knee. When this band thickens, it is known as IT band syndrome. With IT band syndrome, this band rubs against the bone in your knee and it causes inflammation in the area. When you have IT band syndrome, you feel pain, soreness, or irritation on the outside of your knee. You will generally feel this pain or

irritation during and after your run. IT band syndrome is caused by a wide range of different factors. The main cause of IT band syndrome is increasing your mileage too quickly. It can also be caused by weak muscles in the hips and glutes.

How to Prevent IT Band Syndrome

1) Always warm up properly before you start your run. Unfortunately, many runners do not take the time to warm up properly.

2) Try to run on soft surfaces as much as possible, rather than concrete surfaces.

3) If you feel any pain in your knees, then lower your mileage or take a few days off from running.

Heel Pain

When you run, you are placing quite a bit of stress on your heels, which can lead to problems, like heel pain. Many runners experience soreness, pain or irritation on their heels. When you have irritation or swelling on the heels, you will likely feel pain when you put weight on it. This can make running difficult and painful. Heel pain is generally caused by running too much, in shoes that aren't comfortable.

How to Prevent Heel Pain

1) Make sure that you are wearing comfortable running shoes. Ill-fitting or worn running shoes can be uncomfortable, and they can cause heel pain.

2) Run on softer surfaces, rather than concrete. Running on hard surfaces puts more pressure on your heels.

3) Don't increase your mileage too drastically.

Chapter Nine: Training Programs for Running Stronger and Faster

Part of becoming a stronger, faster, and more efficient runner is following a training program. Using a training program or schedule helps you to remain focus and disciplined, and therefore, more likely to achieve your running goals.

A good training program should not only incorporate running, but it should also include strength training, plyometric training, and cross training too. Incorporating different types of exercises into your training program, in addition to running, makes you a better runner overall.

Where stretching, strength, plyometrics and cross training are mentioned in the following training programs, please take exercises from the previous corresponding chapters that you feel best suit your fitness needs. Also, when stretching is mentioned, it is in reference to yoga poses.

Choosing the Right Training Program for your Fitness Level

While it can be tempting to jump straight from the couch to a full marathon, it's not a good idea. Instead, you want to choose a distance to aim for that is more suited to your experience level, before you move onto longer distances. For example, if you are an experienced 5k runner, then work on reaching 10k, but don't jump straight to a half marathon. Similarly, if you are a complete beginner with little to no running experience, then work on reaching 5k, but don't skip straight to 10k.

A 5K Run Explained

Many beginners can't even run a mile, let alone 5K. In a running sense, 5K means 5 kilometers. When talking about a 5K run it is reference to a run that spans 5 kilometers. 5 kilometers is about 3.1 miles and 1 kilometer is about 0.62

miles. The time it takes a person to complete a 5K run will vary, depending on many factors, like fitness level and experience level. For beginners, a 5K run is the perfect distance to aim for, as it is not too long, and it can be worked up to slowly, and steadily. As a beginner, you should never attempt to aim for more than a 5K run. In fact, you should work your way up to a mile first, before you move on.

A 10K Run Explained

A 10k run refers to a run that is 10 kilometers. A 10 kilometer run is about 6.2 miles. More seasoned runners who have experience in 5K runs will aim to complete a 10K run. There are competitive 10k races that runners can enter, but many runners simply aim to run 10k during their general training program. You should not attempt to complete a 10k run unless you have at least completed a 5K run. Even then, you should work up from 5K to 6K to 7K and so on. Increasing your running distance too suddenly can cause you to become injured and overworked.

Training Programs

The following training programs are designed for different experience levels, so ensure that you choose the one that best suits your needs. These training programs are relatively simple. They focus on building up your miles slowly and steadily, so that your body has time to get used to increases in mileage. Don't be tempted to up your mileage too much at once, or you will risk injury.

1. Beginner to 5k Training Program

If you are a beginner when it comes to running, then it's best to train for a 5k run first, before trying to attempt a 10k run or a half marathon. When you are starting out, it's important that you don't try to get ahead of yourself. If you start out too fast, you will only end up injuring yourself, and putting your training schedule behind. Here's a simple 5k training program, which is ideal for beginners.

Stage 1

Duration: 20 Minutes per Day
Schedule: 3 Times per Week

Walk for ten minutes to warm up. Then alternate 1 minute of jogging and 1½ minutes of walking. Do this for twenty minutes in total. When you feel comfortable with this level of exercise, move onto stage two.

Stage 2
Duration: 20 Minutes per Day
Schedule: 3 Times per Week

Walk for ten minutes to warm up. Then, alternate two minutes of walking with two minutes of jogging. Do this for twenty minutes. Again, following this running schedule for as long as you need to before you move onto the next stage.

Stage 3
Duration: 20 Minutes per Day
Schedule: 3 to 5 Times per Week

Start by walking for ten minutes to warm up. Then alternate 3 minutes of jogging with one minute of walking. Do this for twenty minutes. When you feel comfortable with this level of walking, then move onto the next stage of training.

Stage 4
Duration: 30 Minutes per Day
Schedule: 3 to 5 Times per Week

Walk for five minutes to warm up. Jog for 5 to 8 minutes, and then walk for one minute. Alternate this pattern. Do this for 25 to 30 minutes.

Stage 5
Duration: 30 Minutes per Day
Schedule: 3 to 5 Times per Week

Walk for five minutes to warm up. Then jog for 10 minutes, followed by a 1 minute break. Do this for 30 minutes in total. As you progress each day, or each week, try to jog for twenty minutes without a walking break, and then continue building it up until you reach thirty minutes of uninterrupted jogging.

As you gradually increase the time that you run for, you will become fitter, until, you are able to run for thirty minutes, without having to take a break.

2. 5k to 10k Training Program

Being able to complete longer and longer runs is something that all runners strive for. Once you have mastered the 5k run, you then move onto 6k to 10k runs. Again, running is all about taking it slow, and building up your strength and cardio. If you try to rush through, you will injure yourself. Below is a simple program for running 6k to 10k.

Week One:

Mon	Stretch and warm up. Run for 2 miles + Strength or Plyometrics
Tues	Cross Train
Wed	Stretch and warm up. Run for 2 miles
Thurs	Rest
Fri	Strength or Plyometrics + Cross Train
Sat	Rest
Sun	Stretch and warm up. Run for 3 miles.

Week Two:

Mon	Stretch and warm up. Run for 2 miles + Strength or Plyometrics
Tues	Cross Train
Wed	Stretch and warm up. Run for 2.5 miles
Thurs	Rest
Fri	Strength or Plyometrics + Cross Train
Sat	Rest
Sun	Stretch and warm up. Run for 4 miles.

Week Three:

Mon	Stretch and warm up. Run for 2 miles + Strength or

	Plyometrics
Tues	Cross Train
Wed	Stretch and warm up. Run for 3 miles
Thurs	Rest
Fri	Strength or Plyometrics + Cross Train
Sat	Rest
Sun	Stretch and warm up. Run for 4.5 miles.

Week Four:

Mon	Stretch and warm up. Run for 2 miles + Strength or Plyometrics
Tues	Cross Train
Wed	Stretch and warm up. Run for 3 miles
Thurs	Rest
Fri	Strength or Plyometrics + Cross Train
Sat	Rest
Sun	Stretch and warm up. Run for 5 miles.

Week Five:

Mon	Stretch and warm up. Run for 2 miles + Strength or Plyometrics
Tues	Cross Train
Wed	Stretch and warm up. Run for 3 miles
Thurs	Rest
Fri	Strength or Plyometrics + Cross Train
Sat	Rest
Sun	Stretch and warm up. Run for 6 miles.

Week Six:

Mon	Stretch and warm up. Run for 2 miles + Strength or Plyometrics
Tues	Cross Train
Wed	Stretch and warm up. Run for 3 miles
Thurs	Rest
Fri	Strength or Plyometrics + Cross Train
Sat	Rest
Sun	Stretch and warm up. Run for 6.2 miles (10km).

Becoming a stronger, faster, and more efficient runner takes time, patience and discipline. It doesn't happen overnight. By sticking with a training program, and diversifying your training, you can become a better runner and beat your personal best.

Copyright 2014 © Goodlivingbooks Publishing - All rights reserved.

All rights Reserved. No part of this publication or the information in it may be quoted from or reproduced in any form by means such as printing, scanning, photocopying or otherwise without prior written permission of the copyright holder.

Disclaimer and Terms of Use:
Effort has been made to ensure that the information in this book is accurate and complete, however, the author and the publisher do not warrant the accuracy of the information, text and graphics contained within the book due to the rapidly changing nature of science, research, known and unknown facts and internet. The Author and the publisher do not hold any responsibility for errors, omissions or contrary interpretation of the subject matter herein. This book is presented solely for motivational and informational purposes only.

Printed in Great Britain
by Amazon